Poet's Desire

Kathleen Byron Etzel

Contents

Million Miles

Can you feel
My hungry heart
A million miles away
Beating solely for yours
As my night turns to your day?

Gentle Soul

Gentle soul
Of worlds away
To our home
You found your way

Peace and Joy

My soul you've given peace and joy
On this day, my heart to thee
For family, friends, all to see
With deepest love – yours to me
Back to you, that makes three
My vow to you with life anew –
Our bond complete, forever be
As Angels watch from skies above
So, promise, laughter, life and undying love

Weight

My soul is bound
By the singular weight
Of frozen fears

Painful Years

Your eyes shed a single tear
Which displays a river of
Hurt from decades of
Painful years
And yet
And
Yet
Though you never forget
Instead
Persist, then survive
Your spirit protects

More

I have a desire for
Something more

I have a desire for
Something more

Puzzle

Tumultuous complexity
Shifts to
Peaceful simplicity
As pieces of life's
Puzzle slide into place

Insanity

Insanity
Set in
The moment
She let him
Lock the
Door of her
Soul

Connections

When connections reach out of bounds
Of worlds lost not found
Please deliver to me
The love I seek

Engulf

Water engulfed our bodies as
We dove under the surface, our
Weightless hair flowing all around,
Moonlit radiance abound –
A full moon,
Offering enough light to project
Gentle glows and soft shadows.
It was on this magical night,
I fell in love with you

Peak

When I peak out from under the stars
I ponder my life thus far
And so grateful I am your wife
But
If I rewind
I'd leave you far behind
And move ahead
Thinking not with my heart
But rather my head
For life has been less than kind
Based on my own design

Souls know ours it yet to be
The time when destiny
See us as one
For all eternity

Kindness

You can't force love
You can't force respect
But
Kindness –
A word to love by

Trappings

Sounds of sleeting rain
Blanket her mind
With the rat tat tat of refrain
From all that is still in a life
Destined for pain
Released only from trappings
Weighing down souls
That have little to gain
By staying hidden
In the shadows of others inane
Thoughts and worries

Dousing Flame

There's a difference between tame and
Dousing one's flame

The latter won't do
Time to end this ridiculous game

I prefer passions set a blaze
That circles my heart like a whirling dervish
Burning through a
Breamore Mizmaze

Take Hold

Take my hand-
It's okay to let go
And take hold
Of love

Lonely

The loneliest hours
Are at night,
With you
By my side

Sustaining Air

Not to dwell, but this week has been a literal hell
For reason unknow, I have descended into a shell
Yet I have everything going for me, can't you tell?

Let me examine the reasons causing this strife
That has interrupted my flowing life…

The past months have been a mad race –
Out of control some may say – leaving my body behind
My mind to chase.

To hasten my transition, I have valiantly attempted
To firmly implant a new position.

Lovely as love making may be, I have passed up
Each and every opportunity presented to me.

Companionship is nice but not at the cost of sharing
My life with one who means little – that type of
Nurturing is not my device.

Especially when I am in love with one and
I shouldn't be for they're with another, specifically their
Long term lover.

Perhaps in time she'll be mine but until such
An occurrence, a happier time
Will take all endurance
To realize that I am for me

Not the outcome of
Another's paramour.

This I desperately need to discover, however
Linger as I may with this game I continually play.

Their match I couldn't and wouldn't dissolve
Any and all problems are theirs to resolve.

So, you say to me if it were to end,
You'd be there
To quickly snatch?
And I'd say to you,
Yes, of course,
If she's there to catch.

You see the quality which I observe
Is one I longingly deserve.
To substitute would contradict
That which my pride
Has helped to institute
As you may well predict.
Love to me is energy to burn
Sustaining air, I breath
And more priceless than money I earn.

And where does this bring me?
A monogamy for one who isn't even aware I deeply care.
And should that feeling I never disclose,
She is still the one I have chose.

With all the cons
More importantly,

All the pros,
An enduring passion remains
Within each line
I compose.

Lifted Fear

My peace, lay as I rest
Knowing knowledge of thee –
Powers supremely be
Thy utter beauty, lovingly to me.

For a time,
Thy soul,
Blessed in mine,
Purity hold.

Tearless tear
Felt with droplet
Weight
From lifted fear
Of now hateless hate
For open wounds
And gone
This too soon.

Yet love transcends
As tenderness mends.
A gift I see –
Glance ward – back
Horizon's bend
Of setting sun and
Lifting moon,
Again, to give,
Harken noon,
Step – this soon.

For forever
Shall ye be
A spirit which
Allowed grace
Openness free.

Beauty

Love the one
Who sees beauty in
Your scars
And you
In theirs

Delirium

I want to decidedly dive
Into the center of your soul
And drown in the
Delicious delirium
That is you

Heart Leap

When he walked into the room,
A near stranger,
She felt her heart leap
With familiar exhilaration –

Simultaneously,
She knew
She had
Fallen out of love

Silent Fury

Love silent fury
Knowing where you are
Not really
Do I care?
Should I worry?
Lips so soft
Body so fair
What we shared
Gone now
Would never think
Our life together
Filled with care
Never together
As we planned
Life – we've been cheated
As young love
'Tis defeated

Discover

See yourself
Within in a world
 Of those left behind
By humankind
And there you'll find
The subliminal and sublime

Now steady your yourself
To further discover
Another world
Where those around
Are nothing but loving
and oh so kind

Believe

Believe in –
Love
Family
Yourself

Delicacies

A triad of delicacies
Exists in the minds
Of those that let go
And
Fly with the wind

Travel Alone

Sometimes-
Just Sometimes
Your soul
Needs to travel
Alone

Exceptional

Her never ending forward
Determination touched
Individuals close to her and
Those who never knew her
Alike, but will always
Remember her for being
Truly exceptional

Melody

Listen to the melody
Of your soul
And
Feel your heart sing

Mediocrity

Reciprocity creates mediocrity
Of conversations same
When all that is wanted
Are pleasantries
After introductions,
I can never remember anyone's
Name

This certainly shouldn't be so,
For
From all is the potential to gain.

Wolves

Slightly removed from
The howling wolves
That dwell over the hills
And into the forest
I hope for a glimpse
Of the mighty and free
And wonder what life
Would be
Living among my
Loyal pack

Praises

Find the one who
Isn't afraid to sing your
Praises
For all the world
To hear

Winding Ways

Whirling winds whisper
Winding ways of
Guidance
Through
Life's plentiful paths
As your soul listens in
Mindful silence

For you

Reach for the stars
My love,
They shine
For you

Reassess

If someone misses you
Because they don't want
To be alone –
Might be time to reassess your
Relationship

Blazing Memories

Again, rest assure
To breathe a fire pure
Instead of blazing memories
I believe
A salvage need
For grow I shall from
Shallow's way
Blessed soul,
Bring thy day.

Ethereal

Tenderly
Step forward
In motion
With mine
As we begin
Our moonlight
Dance in unified time
With an ethereal clock
Of lover's so long ago

Dreams Sown

Relish I do, the company we keep
While you lay fast asleep
In dreams sown
From worlds unknown
For travel I too
To centuries lived long before
As we fall in love
Forever again.

Poet's Desire

A poet's desire ~ thoughts floated
Onto paper translate into words
Softly spoken in the hush of a
Candle lit evening as tenderly
We lay in each other's dreams
Professing love – our greatest love

Future

In your eyes I see adventure, goodness,
Bravery, laughter, the layers of the world
Revealed through loving kindness,
Acceptance and justice.
I see the future in all you've become and
Strive to be.
I see my world turned around as my
Children are the ones teaching me.
And so, the parenting pendulum of life
Brings me to lessons of love – from child to
Parent to parent to child – an amazing cycle
Of soulful love not even, time can defy

Perfection

Hey that's me
In your
Reflection
Of perfection

I See

Dream with me
Our future I see
Do you too?
Tomorrow will be better
Then before
Because I'll love you so
Much
More

Magnetic Eyes

The most magnificent sunset could
Never match the sensational sunrise
Reflected in your magnetic eyes
As I drown in
The mirage of you

Soothing Soul

Surrender your
Maddening mind
To your
Soothing soul

Ruminations

Oh, heart of mine, the range of
Emotions you must feel as I filter
Ruminations through my mind
But those that you generate are
The ones held dear
For they let me know how
Precious life is far and near

Melancholy

Melancholy roller coasters
Never bolster
One's sense of pride
Rather they can dimmish
One's will to survive

As You Do

In this world,
Love the one that
Loves as you do

Epitaphs

Disastrous decisions
Can decidedly
Change the direction
Set by fate
But wait-
Isn't fate just that,
Deciding our path,
The good and the bad
All laid out on our behalf
With no regrets
Inscribed on our peaceful epitaphs?

Bittersweet

The bittersweet ending
Neither planned
Is seemingly at hand
As one
Fell out of love
From the other
Spellbinding spell

Temporal Spirit

Hurt beyond my
Temporal spirit
Of learned. Learn.

If I let flood,
My soul sadness shake,
If I merely be,
My mind for none,
Not I take.

Waterfall over-wash a mend
To shallow
My maker make
Afraid to say
A name once so
Gentle cuddling
Tame
To brightness same.

If I start,
Shall I stop?
Quivering voice
Hold my thoughts
So none can hear.
Pain I mask
With snapping band;
Laughter to angered fear.
Want I so to feel

Arms of brethren merriment
Holding sum of
Sumless despair.
Time, I pause
With grandiose lose.

Wager my pain
With gentleness came
Thoughts once claimed
Yet emptiness remains
As linger I, in shame,
Over the 'should' profane.

Eyes now close with eternity
Poetics foreshadow,
Glimpse my peace as
Piece my soul,
Relative ingrained.

Moral Pauses

Secular causes
Result in
Moral Pauses

Breath

Fly with the angel
That takes
Your breath away

Sameness

Preputial resistance
Creates
Unrelenting persistence
Of sameness – No?
Yes – but where
Shall we go from here?

Deception

Don't lose yourself
In the
Filtered perception
Of other's
Unknowing deception
For you are
Perfect

Shadows

Resist hiding
Among
The shadows of
Tomorrow

Ebb and Flow

It's Ok with sit
With
The ebb and flow of
Sadness –
You'll be ok

Dream Today

Believe
in your
dreams
today
live them
Tomorrow

Fleeting Memories

Fleeting memories
Threads of tears
Life with peers
From here to there
Throughout the years
Always, Always love
We share

Undying Love

Allow me to you
Undying love

Wonderful

Wonderfully wicked
Are the ways of
Lustful lovers

Artificial

Romance striped
From her soul,
Her love falls
For the rescuing few
Who weave a net of
Artificial adoration
And meaningless trifles
That true love
Simply can't rival

Venture

Mate of Mind
In dreams do bare
Tenderly at night
Embracingly care
The answer you seek
Arises with sleep
As together we venture
Our being to keep

Trumpets Trump

Thunder thump
And pilots jump.
Bugles raise
Now trumpets trump
As unborn rage
Completes a mortal stage
Men less fright
Gory battles fight.

Mother wail
Of battle tails.
Glory be
To take
You took this life from me.
Child, I give and soul return
In bloody earnest urn.

Billions buy
Civilization, why?
When spatter spree
Wounded freedom free
Of mangled bone
Chosen death, atonement tone.

Genius be?
Thy destruction no different
Then they to thee
So, weaponry whip
A lesser ship of foreign sea

Yet dare not cheer
With gleeful glee
As lives, ours lost - -
A single breath - -
Feel the loss
Human lives, pre-tell the cost?
Heads of state
Watchful children emulate.

Flow of Life

Gravity to you
And you to see
The flow of Life
Once more you be

Meaning Beyond My Own

When we met
I dared believe in love
That could give life
Meaning beyond my own
But then I saw
A world I'd never known
Of anger, fear
And tears
That lead me down a path
Of terror that forever I'd part
With my truest heart
Yet now I see that truly
Ours is an echo of life before –
Souls from distant shores
So from you to me and with
Gratitude in all I see
Delicately, deliberately
Love, simply, is always the key

Charmed

With the sweet sounds of
Spring,
Peace floats
Through the evening air
As a charmed nightingale once
Again, regales us all
As she effortlessly
Sings

Blissfully Blinded

I love
being
blissfully blinded
by
your beautiful
being

Utter Despair

Floating among
The mist of
utter despair,
The longest look of love
A glance at fate,
A titling head,
Completely changed
A forlorn state
As she felt her soulmate
Approach
With a single red rose
Signifying eternal
Passionate hope

Sensuous Spell

Oh love,
what sensuous
spell
you cast on me

Blank Mind

My mind's
A blank-
"Tis the beauty of
Your soothing soul
I've so graciously to thank

Sage

Simply stated
A life
She hated
Became the sage
That would further engage
All that would rightly hold
Until she shouted
Let me go!
And with peace in hand
Taken from climates she read,
She escaped the dread
Swirling 'round her head
And now lives
In the harmonious land
Long ago planned
Filled with gentle, kind love
Of same selfless souls
So too choosing
To continuously evolve
Rather than dissolve

Chameleon

Her ever-present façade of grace
Masks a chameleon's
Heart made of lace
All may see what
She conceals –
An inner persona that yearns to
Match her outer glow
Broadcast for a beleaguered show

Tangled Weeds

Rather than
Perch among the tangled
Weeds
Let your thoughts
Fly
Within the limitless Universe
Of endless possibilities

Golden Days

Cherished stories
Of golden days
May well entertain
Our dinner guests
But careful now
To leave the rest –
Their ultimate entertaining test
To resolve on their own
The when, where, how,
The dare

Forevermore

There —in the hypnotic waves
The answers
I once did seek —
I see them too —
For you are mine
And
I be yours
From east to west
And north to south
Lips to mouth
Now sealed from shore to shore
Forevermore

Random Blues

Sunday News
Random blues
Ruffled sheets
Souls that meet
Watching snow
Soothe the sky

Next week
Dancing
Cheek to cheek
Off to Paris
Then to Rome
Wherever we go-
A place
We call home

Protest with Peace

Staggering thoughts
Of Christian vows
Asked her to disavow
Her inner being
So rather than
Change her stand
She left her clan,
Devoted her heart
To another plan
And became a man
For it's not God
Who taught
One to hate –
Protest with peace
It's the least
Anyone can do

Trite

Are you insane?
I ask not to be trite
But I see your fright
As you continually
Live in a world of thoughts
That drive you mad

Not my place to say
But if it were me
Rather than take hate
I'd give
Love a try
Actually, this is what
You say to me
So easy to do
When you find your way

Daughter's

Rest tomorrow
In your daughter's lap
Wrapped with
Gratitude
And grace
For the future
Is hers
To take hold of,
Become a part of,
Then
Astonishingly create

Confound

Predilections for certain dictions
Confound the mind
When those we meet come from
A different side of the street
So, we find
A similar kind
Not in mind
But humankind

Whole

You are us
&
We are you

Home

Celebrate
People that
Feel like
Home

Sanctity Late

Hurt survive
Releasing cry
Love, no hate –
Rather not or sanctity late.
Phase of travel,
To reach, to be
Tis thy fate
Before thy soul
That doth unravel.
Erase a portion,
Least the pain,
Memory still
Though anger,
Thee shan't detain.
Arrive ye shall
From precipice steep:
All that was,
Now dispersed
Bygone with the hardest leap.
A push felt needed?
'Twas thy unconscious
That did leadith,
Tormenting emotions have receded

Crumbling Plaster

Standing before
Winds of eel
Rushed breeze
Ironic, heavenly ease
Bellowing my rhythm
So erupting
Paved catechisms
While
Shattered past
My living cast
Of crumbling plaster

Whisper Weep

Scared to sleep?
Dared soul,
She'd keep—
Or,
Fearful heavenly whisper weep?

Harpsichord Bliss

A picture paints
Only to taint
With reality's
Shadowy wrath
Of benevolence
Unto a kindly behalf.
Latent fears
Of shielded cheers.
Perceive my view –
'Tis what I see,
Perception of miss
Of you.
Harpsichord bliss,
Sorrow gone,
'Tis dismissed
For organ pangs
Open. my mouth
Outrageously grown fangs.

Take my side,
My internal being.
Together we shall ride,
Smothering the sap,
Runneth deep,
Brush thy lap
Of petals draped,
Cut the ribbon
Loosely tapped.

Grow from a lass,
Nightly allowance
Of undue harass.
'Tis you who brought
Tooth and nail,
Of lovers fraught.
Life of rage,
Another page?
Or expulsion rumble
As rapids run,
Someday my demon
Shall be done.

Faint

Heart and face
Who survives with pittance?
A fly?
Why, once did I?

'Tis my fool I most despise
But recovery shall mend
From casual reprisal
Until artist paint
Kindly felt but respectfully faint.

Calamity

I realize the insanity
Behind this enduring calamity –
What am I to do?
For silently I long
But certainly not pursue

Purple Shades

As do you,
Longingly, faithfully, I renew
Beautiful essence within
Passion relinquished of sin
Perpetually filled days
An enigma of purple shades
Thy being of thy heart once set
Asunder my spirit, this day without -
Never to start or reset

Emotional Demise

Why express my life to you?
Certainly, so in times
Of emotional demise
Beyond all other contacts
Is beyond my concept
Whatever the outcome maybe,
My expression of eternal
Gratitude within my
Unspoken love;
Tender as I may feel,
Though this shouldn't be so,
Seldom do I reveal

Crisp Night

Benches set in snow,
Evening stars a glow.
Cold crisp night
Of friend and foe
Take my hand,
Single my finger
Shivering pulse
To but a linger.
Die the day;
My what may
Change dismay
Clouds of mindless fray.

Hang a hum
With thy shivering tongue.
What if I turn away
Never to receive that once wanted.
Happier in the end
Now I feel
Yet only tomorrow shall reveal.

Before us tis the living;
I shan't have a solitary misgiving.
For what hath given me all that tis
In life's distant memory

Internal Concepts

Here we met again in order to descend to the
Depths of internal concepts.

A balance between the glowing and brilliant gleam
Disallow all eternal vows, what my heart says won't
Escape me now.

Don't dismiss a friendly kiss as one of innocence,
But rather permit the true passion from which it
Emits.

Tender as it may seem, my dreams conjure a different
Scene.
Meaning the delivery is sensual and really
Quite intentional.

As you can see, the innocence lies in the disbelief
That manifestation is
Beyond my reach.
But such a want is a matter of the heart
which my mind does taunt.

For whatever the outcome, once again, I ponder
As I continually grow fonder
Of the beauty you bestow
And your enamored glow

Checkmate

How should I know –
Love does yours continue to grow?

Of course, why my doubt?
Or is there reason,
I want out.

Don't take that wrong
My intensity still great-
Queens of spades, checkmate
Love games
Shall I wait?

My fate I watch as the sun does set,
But you with
Yourself have yet met.

So now I sit with bewilderment twitch.

No matter what's yours, the time is late.
A minute gone by-
I believe I shall, must vacate
Our lifelong date.

Anew

Surely love will win
And we can begin
Our life anew

www.ingramcontent.com/pod-product-compliance
Lightning Source LLC
Chambersburg PA
CBHW031349160726
47993CB00002B/894